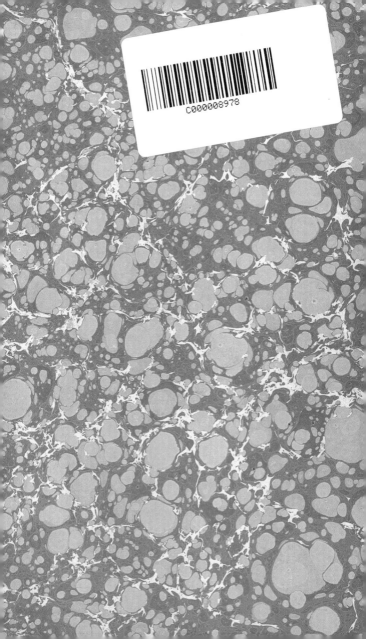

THE ILLUSTRATED POETS

Acts 1v.9,10.

THE ILLUSTRATED POETS

Gerard Manley Hopkins

Selected and with an introduction
by Geoffrey Moore

AURUM PRESS

First published 1993 by Aurum Press Ltd,
25 Bedford Avenue, London WC1B 3AT
Selection and introduction copyright © 1993 by Geoffrey Moore

A catalogue record for this book is available
from the British Library

ISBN 1 85410 257 5

2 4 6 8 10 9 7 5 3 1
1994 1996 1997 1995 1993

Picture research by Juliet Brightmore

Typeset by Computerset, Harmondsworth, Middlesex
Printed in Hong Kong by Imago

CONTENTS

INTRODUCTION

Gerard Manley Hopkins was born at Stratford in Essex, on 28 July 1844, the eldest of nine children. His father was head of a firm of marine insurance brokers, but he showed a great interest in literature, inherited by his son who won Highgate School's Poetry Prize with 'The Escorial' when he was only 16. From Highgate Gerard went as an Exhibitioner to Balliol College, Oxford. At this stage it would be fair to call him a Pre-Raphaelite, for his ambition was to be both a painter and a poet, like Dante Gabriel Rossetti. He was attracted to the writings of Ruskin and Pater but was increasingly drawn to the Oxford Movement. Inevitably, he came under the powerful influence of John Henry (later Cardinal) Newman.

In October 1866 Hopkins was received into the Catholic church and a poem of this year, 'The Habit of Perfection', shows how strong was his attraction to the priesthood. When he obtained a First in Greats, Newman invited him to teach at the Oratory School in Edgbaston. In 1868 he entered the Society of Jesus and either taught, or was a priest, in Wales and at Liverpool, Glasgow, Stonyhurst and elsewhere. In 1884 he was made Professor of Classics at University College, Dublin, but after 5 years of poor health he died of typhoid fever at the age of 45.

The history of Gerard Manley Hopkins's poetic reputation is akin to that of Emily Dickinson. Both were born in the first half of the nineteenth century; both were strongly influenced by the Christian religion; both were virtually unpublished in their lifetime. Finally, both had their work brought to public attention through the good offices of a friend.

In the case of Hopkins the friend was Robert Bridges,

later to be Poet Laureate. Bridges was quick to sense the uniqueness of Hopkins's talent, if not brave enough to publish his friend's work until nearly 30 years after his death. By 1918, after the new broom of the First World War, he felt that the time was ripe.

He was correct. Wilfred Owen's justifiable cynicism had negated the boyish patriotism of Rupert Brooke, and Yeats had turned to the bare new style of 'Easter 1916'. The poems of T.S. Eliot, William Carlos Williams and Wallace Stevens had been appearing in magazines for some years. In this atmosphere, the verse experiments of the Victorian Hopkins caught the imagination of the more far-sighted critics. Not the bulk of the poetry-reading public, though; it took ten years for Bridges' scholarly edition of 750 copies to sell out. Then, in the age of Auden, there was a revival of interest; in 1930 Charles Williams edited a second edition. Finally, in 1948, W.H. Gardner brought out the third, enlarged edition which was to establish Hopkins as a major poet.

As Pound was fond of pointing out, the traditional measure of English verse for the past 400 years had been iambic. When the music of Chaucer triumphed over the stave-beat of Langland, the stage was set for a kind of poetry which flowed magnificently in the work of Shakespeare, Marlowe and Milton. The first breach in what T.S. Eliot called 'the Chinese Wall of Milton' was made by Wordsworth. But Wordsworth's achievement – as Whitman was later to say of his own work – was in the nature of a 'language experiment'. Hopkins was more interested in metrics. With an ear attuned to the rhythms of Middle English and Welsh metres he turned away from the Latin-French measures which dominated English poetry – from 'running rhythm' to 'sprung rhythm'.

By sprung rhythm Hopkins meant the stressing of certain strong syllables 'naturally', as in ordinary speech, and the gathering into their orbit of other, slack, syllables, which he called 'outrides'. For example, the first two lines of Hopkins's most famous poem, 'The Windhover', yield five 'sprung' or heavily-stressed syllables with the slack syllables caught up in the main stress pattern. The heavy stresses are indicated by acute accents:

I cáught this mórning mórning's mínion, kíng-
dom of dáylight's dáuphin, dapple-dáwn-drawn Fálcon,
    in his ríding . . .

Hopkins invented other words to describe his highly individual approach to poetry. 'Inscape' was his term for what Duns Scotus called the 'haeccitas' or 'thisness' of an object or scene, its innate, essential quality. 'Instress' is the power that holds inscape together.

Hopkins's poetry is all strength and energy. His dislocated syllables are instinct with an effort to communicate the power of his often anguished thought and feeling. In fact, T.S. Eliot's term for the achievement of the Metaphysical poets, 'felt thought', would not be inapt to describe that same 'drawing together of disparate elements' which creates for Hopkins the flash of 'inscape'. Above all he sought to avoid, with great success, what he called the 'Parnassian' style – that is, poeticizing without inspiration. No poet could have put more of himself into his work and the reader who immerses himself in what at first seems a strange and difficult way of writing is made alive with an acute awareness of the glory of the world.

GEOFFREY MOORE

Myself unholy, from myself unholy
To the sweet living of my friends I look –
Eye-greeting doves bright-counter to the rook,
Fresh brooks to salt sand-teasing waters shoaly: –
And they are purer, but alas! not solely
The unquestion'd readings of a blotless book.
And so my trust, confusèd, struck, and shook
Yields to the sultry siege of melancholy.
He has a sin of mine, he its near brother;
Knowing them well I can but see the fall.
This fault in one I found, that in another:
And so, though each have one while I have all,
No *better* serves me now, save *best*; no other
Save Christ: to Christ I look, on Christ I call.

Heaven-Haven

A nun takes the veil

I have desired to go
    Where springs not fail,
To fields where flies no sharp and sided hail
    And a few lilies blow.

And I have asked to be
    Where no storms come,
Where the green swell is in the havens dumb,
    And out of the swing of the sea.

Let me be to Thee as the circling bird,
Or bat with tender and air-crisping wings
That shapes in half-light his departing rings,
From both of whom a changeless note is heard.
I have found my music in a common word,
Trying each pleasurable throat that sings
And every praisèd sequence of sweet strings,
And know infallibly which I preferred.
The authentic cadence was discovered late
Which ends those only strains that I approve,
And other science all gone out of date
And minor sweetness scarce made mention of:
I have found the dominant of my range and state –
Love, O my God, to call Thee Love and Love.

The Habit of Perfection

Elected Silence, sing to me
And beat upon my whorlèd ear,
Pipe me to pastures still and be
The music that I care to hear.

Shape nothing, lips; be lovely-dumb:
It is the shut, the curfew sent
From there where all surrenders come
Which only makes you eloquent.

Be shellèd, eyes, with double dark
And find the uncreated light:
This ruck and reel which you remark
Coils, keeps, and teases simple sight.

Palate, the hutch of tasty lust,
Desire not to be rinsed with wine:
The can must be so sweet, the crust
So fresh that come in fasts divine!

Nostrils, your careless breath that spend
Upon the stir and keep of pride,
What relish shall the censers send
Along the sanctuary side!

O feel-of-primrose hands, O feet
That want the yield of plushy sward,
But you shall walk the golden street
And you unhouse and house the Lord.

And, Poverty, be thou the bride
And now the marriage feast begun,
And lily-coloured clothes provide
Your spouse not laboured-at nor spun.

The Wreck of the Deutschland

To the
happy memory of five Franciscan nuns
exiles by the Falck Laws
drowned between midnight and morning of
Dec. 7th, 1875

PART THE FIRST

1

Thou mastering me
God! giver of breath and bread;
World's strand, sway of the sea;
Lord of living and dead;
Thou has bound bones and veins in me, fastened me flesh,
And after it almost unmade, what with dread,
Thy doing: and dost thou touch me afresh?
Over again I feel thy finger and find thee.

2

I did say yes
O at lightning and lashed rod;
Thou heardst me truer than tongue confess
Thy terror, O Christ, O God;
Thou knowest the walls, altar and hour and night:
The swoon of a heart that the sweep and the hurl of thee
trod
Hard down with a horror of height:
And the midriff astrain with leaning of, laced with fire of stress.

3

The frown of his face
Before me, the hurtle of hell
Behind, where, where was a, where was a place?
I whirled out wings that spell
And fled with a fling of the heart to the heart of the Host.
My heart, but you were dovewinged, I can tell,
Carrier-witted, I am bold to boast,
To flash from the flame to the flame then, tower from the grace
to the grace.

4

I am soft sift
In an hourglass – at the wall
Fast, but mined with a motion, a drift,
And it crowds and it combs to the fall;
I steady as a water in a well, to a poise, to a pane,
But roped with, always, all the way down from the tall
Fells or flanks of the voel, a vein
Of the gospel proffer, a pressure, a principle, Christ's gift.

5

I kiss my hand
To the stars, lovely-asunder
Starlight, wafting him out of it; and
Glow, glory in thunder;
Kiss my hand to the dapple-with-damson west:
Since, tho' he is under the world's splendour and wonder,
His mystery must be instressed, stressed;
For I greet him the days I meet him, and bless when I
understand.

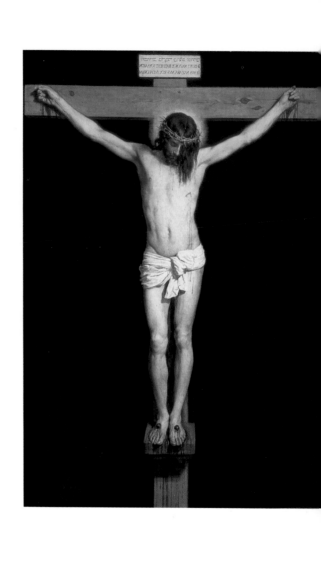

6

Not out of his bliss
Springs the stress felt
Not first from heaven (and few know this)
Swings the stroke dealt –
Stroke and a stress that stars and storms deliver,
That guilt is hushed by, hearts are flushed by and melt –
But it rides time like riding a river
(And here the faithful waver, the faithless fable and miss).

7

It dates from day
Of his going in Galilee;
Warm-laid grave of a womb-life grey;
Manger, maiden's knee;
The dense and the driven Passion, and frightful sweat:
Thence the discharge of it, there its swelling to be,
Though felt before, though in high flood yet –
What none would have known of it, only the heart, being hard
    at bay,

8

Is out with it! Oh,
We lash with the best or worst
Word last! How a lush-kept plush-capped sloe
Will, mouthed to flesh-burst,
Gush! – flush the man, the being with it, sour or sweet,
Brim, in a flash, full! – Hither then, last or first,
To hero of Calvary, Christ's feet –
Never ask if meaning it, wanting it, warned of it – men go.

9

Be adored among men,
God, three-numberèd form;
Wring thy rebel, dogged in den,
Man's malice, with wrecking and storm.
Beyond saying sweet, past telling of tongue,
Thou art lightning and love, I found it, a winter and warm;
Father and fondler of heart thou hast wrung:
Hast thy dark descending and most art merciful then.

10

With an anvil-ding
And with fire in him forge thy will
Or rather, rather then, stealing as Spring
Through him, melt him but master him still:
Whether at once, as once at a crash Paul,
Or as Austin, a lingering-out swéet skíll,
Make mercy in all of us, out of us all
Mastery, but be adored, but be adored King.

PART THE SECOND

11

'Some find me a sword; some
The flange and the rail; flame,
Fang, or flood' goes Death on drum,
And storms bugle his fame.
But wé dream we are rooted in earth – Dust!
Flesh falls within sight of us, we, though our flower the same,
Wave with the meadow, forget that there must
The sour scythe cringe, and the blear share come.

12

On Saturday sailed from Bremen,
American-outward-bound,
Take settler and seamen, tell men with women,
Two hundred souls in the round –
O Father, not under thy feathers nor ever as guessing
The goal was a shoal, of a fourth the doom to be drowned;
Yet did the dark side of the bay of thy blessing
Not vault them, the million of rounds of thy mercy not reeve
even them in?

13

Into the snows she sweeps,
Hurling the haven behind,
The Deutschland, on Sunday; and so the sky keeps,
For the infinite air is unkind,
And the sea flint-flake, black-backed in the regular blow,
Sitting Eastnortheast, in cursed quarter, the wind;
Wiry and white-fiery and whirlwind-swivellèd snow
Spins to the widow-making unchilding unfathering deeps.

14

She drove in the dark to leeward,
She struck – not a reef or a rock
But the combs of a smother of sand: night drew her
Dead to the Kentish Knock;
And she beat the bank down with her bows and the ride of
her keel;
The breakers rolled on her beam with ruinous shock;
And canvas and compass, the whorl and the wheel
Idle for ever to waft her or wind her with, these she endured.

Hope had grown grey hairs,
Hope had mourning on,
Trenched with tears, carved with cares,
Hope was twelve hours gone;
And frightful a nightfall folded rueful a day
Nor rescue, only rocket and lightship, shone,
And lives at last were washing away:
To the shrouds they took, – they shook in the hurling and
horrible airs.

16

One stirred from the rigging to save
The wild woman-kind below,
With a rope's end round the man, handy and brave –
He was pitched to his death at a blow,
For all his dreadnought breast and braids of thew:
They could tell him for hours, dandled the to and fro
Through the cobbled foam-fleece. What could he do
With the burl of the fountains of air, buck and the flood of the
wave?

17

They fought with God's cold –
And they could not and fell to the deck
(Crushed them) or water (and drowned them) or rolled
With the sea-romp over the wreck.
Night roared, with the heart-break hearing a heart-broke
rabble,
The woman's wailing, the crying of child without check –
Till a lioness arose breasting the babble,
A prophetess towered in the tumult, a virginal tongue told.

Ah, touched in your bower of bone,
    Are you! turned for an exquisite smart,
Have you! make words break from me here all alone,
    Do you! – mother of being in me, heart.
O unteachably after evil, but uttering truth,
    Why, tears! is it? tears; such a melting, a madrigal start!
        Never-eldering revel and river of youth,
What can it be, this glee? the good you have there of your own?

Sister, a sister calling
    A master, her master and mine! –
And the inboard seas run swirling and hawling;
    The rash smart sloggering brine
Blinds her; but she that weather sees one thing, one;
Has one fetch in her: she rears herself to divine
    Ears, and the call of the tall nun
To the men in the tops and the tackle rode over the storm's
    brawling.

She was first of a five and came
    Of a coifèd sisterhood.
(O Deutschland, double a desperate name!
    O world wide of its good!
But Gertrude, lily, and Luther, are two of a town,
    Christ's lily and beast of the waste wood:
        From life's dawn it is drawn down,
Abel is Cain's brother and breasts they have sucked the same.)

21

Loathed for a love men knew in them,
Banned by the land of their birth,
Rhine refused them, Thames would ruin them;
Surf, snow, river and earth
Gnashed: but thou art above, thou Orion of light;
Thy unchancelling poising palms were weighing the worth,
Thou martyr-master: in thy sight
Storm flakes were scroll-leaved flowers, lily showers – sweet
heaven was astrew in them.

22

Five! the finding and sake
And cipher of suffering Christ.
Mark, the mark is of man's make
And the word of it Sacrificed.
But he scores it in scarlet himself on his own bespoken,
Before-time-taken, dearest prizèd and priced –
Stigma, signal, cinquefoil token
For lettering of the lamb's fleece, ruddying of the rose-flake.

23

Joy fall to thee, father Francis,
Drawn to the Life that died;
With the gnarls of the nails in thee, niche of the
lance, his
Lovescape crucified
And seal of his seraph-arrival! and these thy daughters
And five-livèd and leavèd favour and pride,
Are sisterly sealed in wild waters,
To bathe in his fall-gold mercies, to breathe in his all-fire
glances.

Away in the loveable west,
On a pastoral forehead of Wales,
I was under a roof here, I was at rest,
And they the prey of the gales;
She to the black-about air, to the breaker, the thickly
Falling flakes, to the throng that catches and quails
Was calling 'O Christ, Christ, come quickly':
The cross to her she calls Christ to her, christens her wild-worst
Best.

25

The majesty! what did she mean?
Breathe, arch and original Breath.
Is it love in her of the being as her lover had been?
Breathe, body of lovely Death.
They were else-minded then, altogether, the men
Woke thee with a *We are perishing* in the weather of
Gennesareth.
Or is it that she cried for the crown then,
The keener to come at the comfort for feeling the combating
keen?

26

For how to the heart's cheering
The down-dugged ground-hugged grey
Hovers off, the jay-blue heavens appearing
Of pied and peeled May!
Blue-beating and hoary-glow height; or night, still higher,
With belled fire and the moth-soft Milky Way,
What by your measure is the heaven of desire,
The treasure never eyesight got, nor was ever guessed what for
the hearing?

27

No, but it was not these.
The jading and jar of the cart,
Time's tasking, it is fathers that asking for ease
Of the sodden-with-its-sorrowing heart,
Not danger, electrical horror; then further it finds
The appealing of the Passion is tenderer in prayer apart:
Other, I gather, in measure her mind's
Burden, in wind's burly and beat of endragonèd seas.

28

But how shall I . . . make me room there:
Reach me a . . . Fancy, come faster –
Strike you the sight of it? look at it loom there,
Thing that she . . . There then! the Master,
Ipse, the only one, Christ, King, Head:
He was to cure the extremity where he had cast her;
Do, deal, lord it with living and dead;
Let him ride, her pride, in his triumph, despatch and have done
with his doom there.

29

Ah! there was a heart right!
There was single eye!
Read the unshapeable shock night
And knew the who and the why;
Wording it how but by him that present and past,
Heaven and earth are word of, worded by? –
The Simon Peter of a soul! to the blast
Tarpeïan-fast, but a blown beacon of light.

Jesu, heart's light,
Jesu, maid's son,
What was the feast followed the night
Thou hadst glory of this nun? –
Feast of the one woman without stain.
For so conceivèd so to conceive thee is done;
But here was heart-throe, birth of a brain,
Word, that heard and kept thee and uttered thee outright.

31

Well, she has thee for the pain, for the
Patience; but pity of the rest of them!
Heart, go and bleed at a bitterer vein for the
Comfortless unconfessed of them –
No not uncomforted: lovely-felicitous Providence
Finger of a tender of, O of a feathery delicacy, the breast of th
Maiden could obey so, be a bell to, ring of it, and
Startle the poor sheep back! is the shipwrack then a harvest,
does tempest carry the grain for thee?

32

I admire thee, master of the tides,
Of the Yore-flood, of the year's fall;
The recurb and the recovery of the gulf's sides,
The girth of it and the wharf of it and the wall;
Stanching, quenching ocean of a motionable mind;
Ground of being, and granite of it: past all
Grasp God, throned behind
Death with a sovereignty that heeds but hides, bodes but abides;

With a mercy that outrides
The all of water, an ark
For the listener; for the lingerer with a love glides
Lower than death and the dark;
A vein for the visiting of the past-prayer, pent in prison,
The-last-breath penitent spirits – the uttermost mark
Our passion-plungèd giant risen,
The Christ of the Father compassionate, fetched in the storm of
his strides.

34

Now burn, new born to the world,
Double-naturèd name,
The heaven-flung, heart-fleshed, maiden-furled
Miracle-in-Mary-of-flame,
Mid-numberèd he in three of the thunder-throne!
Not a dooms-day dazzle in his coming nor dark as he came;
Kind, but royally reclaiming his own;
A released shower, let flash to the shire, not a ligtning of fire
hard-hurled.

35

Dame, at our door
Drowned, and among our shoals,
Remember us in the roads, the heaven-haven of the
reward:
Our King back, Oh, upon English souls!
Let him easter in us, be a dayspring to the dimness of us, be
a crimson-cresseted east,
More brightening her, rare-dear Britain, as his reign rolls,
Pride, rose, prince, hero of us, high-priest,
Our hearts' charity's hearth's fire, our thoughts' chivalry's
throng's Lord.

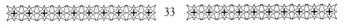

Pied Beauty

Glory be to God for dappled things –
  For skies of couple-colour as a brinded cow;
    For rose-moles all in stipple upon trout that
      swim;
Fresh-firecoal chestnut-falls; finches' wings;
  Landscape plotted and pieced – fold, fallow, and
      plough;
    And áll trádes, their gear and tackle and trim.
All things counter, original, spare, strange;
  Whatever is fickle, freckled (who knows how?)
    With swift, slow; sweet, sour; adazzle, dim;
He fathers-forth whose beauty is past change:
                    Praise him.

God's Grandeur

The world is charged with the grandeur of God.
  It will flame out, like shining from shook foil;
  It gathers to a greatness, like the ooze of oil
Crushed. Why do men then now not reck his rod?
Generations have trod, have trod, have trod;
  And all is seared with trade; bleared, smeared
    with toil;
  And wears man's smudge and shares man's
    smell: the soil
Is bare now, nor can foot feel, being shod.

And for all this, nature is never spent;
  There lives the dearest freshness deep down
      things;
And though the last lights off the black West went
  Oh, morning, at the brown brink eastward,
      springs –
Because the Holy Ghost over the bent
  World broods with warm breast and with ah!
      bright wings

The Starlight Night

Look at the stars! look, look up at the skies!
  O look at all the fire-folk sitting in the air!
  The bright boroughs, the circle-citadels there!
Down in dim woods the diamond delves! the
      elves'-eyes!
The grey lawns cold where gold, where quickgold lies!
  Wind-beat whitebeam! airy abeles set on a flare!
  Flake-doves sent floating forth at a farmyard
      scare! –
Ah well! it is all a purchase, all is a prize.

Buy then! bid then! – What? – Prayer, patience,
      alms, vows.
Look, look: a May-mess, like on orchard boughs!
  Look! March-bloom, like on mealed-with-
      yellow sallows!
These are indeed the barn; withindoors house
The shocks. This piece-bright paling shuts the
      spouse
  Christ home, Christ and his mother and all his
      hallows.

Hurrahing in Harvest

Summer ends now; now, barbarous in beauty, the
    stooks rise
Around; up above, what wind-walks! what lovely
    behaviour
Of silk-sack clouds! has wilder, wilful-wavier
Meal-drift moulded ever and melted across skies?

I walk, I lift up, I lift up heart, eyes,
Down all that glory in the heavens to glean our
    Saviour;
And, éyes, heárt, what looks, what lips yet gave
    you a
Rapturous love's greeting of realer, of rounder
    replies?

And the azurous hung hills are his world-wielding
    shoulder
Majestic – as a stallion stalwart, very-violet-sweet! –
These things, these things were here and but the
    beholder
Wanting; which two when they once meet,
The heart rears wings bold and bolder
And hurls for him, O half hurls earth for him off
    under his feet.

Spring

Nothing is so beautiful as Spring –
   When weeds, in wheels, shoot long and lovely
      and lush;
   Thrush's eggs look little low heavens, and thrush
Through the echoing timber does so rinse and
     wring
The ear, it strikes like lightnings to hear him sing;
   The glassy peartree leaves and blooms, they brush
   The descending blue; that blue is all in a rush
With richness; the racing lambs too have fair their
     fling.

What is all this juice and all this joy?
   A strain of the earth's sweet being in the
     beginning
In Eden garden. – Have, get, before it cloy.

   Before it cloud, Christ, lord, and sour with
     sinning,
Innocent mind and Mayday in girl and boy,
   Most, O maid's child, thy choice and worthy
     the winning.

The Windhover:

To Christ our Lord

I caught this morning morning's minion, king-
  dom of daylight's dauphin, dapple-dawn-drawn
      Falcon, in his riding
  Of the rolling level underneath him steady air,
      and striding
High there, how he rung upon the rein of a
      wimpling wing
In his ecstasy! then off, off forth on swing,
  As a skate's heel sweeps smooth on a bow-bend:
      the hurl and gliding
  Rebuffed the big wind. My heart in hiding
Stirred for a bird, – the achieve of, the mastery of
      the thing!

Brute beauty and valour and act, oh, air, pride,
      plume, here
  Buckle! AND the fire that breaks from thee then,
      a billion
Times told lovelier, more dangerous, O my
      chevalier!

No wonder of it: shéer plód makes plough down
      sillion
Shine, and blue-bleak embers, ah my dear,
  Fall, gall themselves, and gash gold-vermilion.

Binsey Poplars

felled 1879

My aspens dear, whose airy cages quelled,
Quelled or quenched in leaves the leaping sun,
All felled, felled, are all felled;
    Of a fresh and following folded rank
        Not spared, not one
        That dandled a sandalled
     Shadow that swam or sank
On meadow and river and wind-wandering weed-
    winding bank.

O if we but knew what we do
      When we delve or hew –
   Hack and rack the growing green!
      Since country is so tender
   To touch, her being só slender,
   That, like this sleek and seeing ball
   But a prick will make no eye at all,
   Where we, even where we mean
       To mend her we end her,
   When we hew or delve:
After-comers cannot guess the beauty been.
   Ten or twelve, only ten or twelve
     Strokes of havoc únselve
     The sweet especial scene,
    Rural scene, a rural scene,
    Sweet especial rural scene.

The Caged Skylark

As a dare-gale skylark scanted in a dull cage
　　Man's mounting spirit in his bone-house, mean
　　　　house, dwells –
　　That bird beyond the remembering his free fells,
This in drudgery, day-labouring-out life's age.

Though aloft on turf or perch or poor low stage,
　　Both sing sometímes the sweetest, sweetest
　　　　spells,
　　Yet both droop deadly sómetimes in their cells
Or wring their barriers in burst of fear or rage.

Not that the sweet-fowl, song-fowl, needs no rest –
Why, hear him, hear him babble and drop down
　　　　to his nest,
　　But his own nest, wild nest, no prison.

Man's spirit will be flesh-bound when found at
　　　　best,
But uncumberèd: meadow-down is not distressed
　　For a rainbow footing it nor he for his bónes rísen.

Duns Scotus's Oxford

Towery city and branchy between towers;
Cuckoo-echoing, bell-swarmèd, lark-charmèd,
    rook-racked, river-rounded;
The dapple-eared lily below thee; that country and
    town did
Once encounter in, here coped and poisèd powers;

Thou hast a base and brickish skirt there, sours
That neighbour-nature thy grey beauty is grounded
Best in; graceless growth, thou hast confounded
Rural rural keeping – folk, flocks, and flowers.

Yet ah! this air I gather and I release
He lived on; these weeds and waters, these walls
    are what
He haunted who of all men most sways my spirits
    to peace;

Of realty the rarest-veinèd unraveller; a not
Rivalled insight, be rival Italy or Greece;
Who fired France for Mary without spot.

Felix Randal

Felix Randal the farrier, O is he dead then? my
    duty all ended,
Who have watched his mould of man, big-boned
    and hardy-handsome
Pining, pining, till time when reason rambled in it
    and some
Fatal four disorders, fleshed there, all contended?

Sickness broke him. Impatient, he cursed at first,
    but mended
Being anointed and all; though a heavenlier heart
    began some
Months earlier, since I had our sweet reprieve and
    ransom
Tendered to him. Ah well, God rest him all road
    ever he offended!

This seeing the sick endears them to us, us too it
    endears.
My tongue had taught thee comfort, touch had
    quenched thy tears,
Thy tears that touched my heart, child, Felix,
    poor Felix Randal;

How far from then forethought of, all thy more
    boisterous years,
When thou at the random grim forge, powerful
    amidst peers,
Didst fettle for the great grey drayhorse his bright
    and battering sandal!

As kingfishers catch fire, dragonflies draw flame;
　　As tumbled over rim in roundy wells
　　Stones ring; like each tucked string tells, each
　　　　hung bell's
Bow swung finds tongue to fling out broad its name;
Each mortal thing does one thing and the same:
　　Deals out that being indoors each one dwells;
Selves — goes itself; *myself* it speaks and spells,
Crying *What I do is me: for that I came.*

Í say more: the just man justices;
　　Keeps gráce: thát keeps all his going graces;
Acts in God's eye what in God's eye he is —
　　Chríst. For Christ plays in ten thousand places,
Lovely in limbs, and lovely in eyes not his
　　To the Father through the features of men's faces.

Inversnaid

This darksome burn, horseback brown,
His rollrock highroad roaring down,
In coop and in comb the fleece of his foam
Flutes and low to the lake falls home.

A windpuff-bonnet of fáwn-fróth
Turns and twindles over the broth
Of a pool so pitchblack, féll-frówning,
It rounds and rounds Despair to drowning.

Degged with dew, dappled with dew
Are the groins of the braes that the brook treads
    through,
Wiry heathpacks, flitches of fern,
And the beadbonny ash that sits over the burn.

What would the world be, once bereft
Of wet and of wildness? Let them be left,
O let them be left, wildness and wet;
Long live the weeds and the wilderness yet.

Spring and Fall:

to a young child

Márgarét, áre you gríeving
Over Goldengrove unleaving?
Leáves, líke the things of man, you
With your fresh thoughts care for, can you?
Áh! ás the heart grows older
It will come to such sights colder
By and by, nor spare a sigh
Though worlds of wanwood leafmeal lie;
And yet you *will* weep and know why.
Now no matter, child, the name:
Sórrow's spríngs áre the same.
Nor mouth had, no nor mind, expressed
What heart heard of, ghost guessed:
It ís the blight man was born for,
It is Margaret you mourn for.

The Leaden Echo and the
Golden Echo

(Maidens' song from St. Winefred's Well)

THE LEADEN ECHO

How to kéep – is there ány way, is there none
    such, nowhere known some, bow or brooch
    or braid or brace, láce, latch or catch or key
    to keep
Back beauty, keep it, beauty, beauty, beauty, . . .
    from vanishing away?
O is there no frowning of these wrinkles, rankèd
    wrinkles deep,
Down? no waving off of these most mournful
    messengers, still messengers, sad and stealing
    messengers of grey? –
No there's none, there's none, O no there's none,
Nor can you long be, what you now are, called fair,
Do what you may do, what, do what you may,
And wisdom is early to despair:
Be beginning; since, no, nothing can be done
To keep at bay
Age and age's evils, hoar hair,
Ruck and wrinkle, drooping, dying, death's worst,
    winding sheets, tombs and worms and
    tumbling to decay;
So be beginning, be beginning to despair.
O there's none; no no no there's none:
Be beginning to despair, to despair,
Despair, despair, despair, despair.

Spare!

There ís one, yes I have one (Hush there!),
Only not within seeing of the sun.
Not within the singeing of the strong sun,
Tall sun's tingeing, or treacherous the tainting of
    the earth's air,
Somewhere elsewhere there is ah well where! one,
Ońe. Yes I cán tell such a key, I dó know such a
    place,
Where whatever's prizèd and passes of us,
    everything that's fresh and fast flying of us,
    seems to us sweet of us and swiftly away with,
    done away with, undone,
Undone, done with, soon done with, and yet
    dearly and dangerously sweet
Of us, the wimpled-water-dimpled, not-by-
    morning-matchèd face,
The flower of beauty, fleece of beauty, too too apt
    to, ah! to fleet,
Never fleets móre, fastened with the tenderest truth
To its own best being and its loveliness of youth: it
    is an everlastingness of, O it is an all youth!
Come then, your ways and airs and looks, locks,
    maidengear, gallantry and gaiety and grace,
Winning ways, airs innocent, maiden manners,
    sweet looks, loose locks, long locks,
    lovelocks, gaygear, going gallant, girlgrace –
Resign them, sign them, seal them, send them,
    motion them with breath,

And with sighs soaring, soaring síghs, deliver
Them; beauty-in-the-ghost, deliver it, early now,
    long before death
Give beauty back, beauty, beauty, beauty, back to
    God, beauty's self and beauty's giver.
See; not a hair is, not an eyelash, not the least
    lash lost; every hair
Is, hair of the head, numbered.
Nay, what we had lighthanded left in surly the
    mere mould
Will have waked and have waxed and have walked
    with the wind what while we slept,
This side, that side hurling a heavyheaded
    hundredfold
What while we, while we slumbered.
O then, weary then whý should we tread? O why
    are we so haggard at the heart, so care-coiled,
    care-killed, so fagged, so fashed, so cogged, so
    cumbered,
When the thing we freely fórfeit is kept with
    fonder a care,
Fonder a care kept than we could have kept it, kept
Far with fonder a care (and we, we should have
    lost it) finer, fonder
A care kept. – Where kept? do but tell us where
    kept, where. –
Yonder. – What high as that! We follow, now we
    follow. – Yonder, yes yonder, yonder,
Yonder.

Carrion Comfort

Not, I'll not, carrion comfort, Despair, not feast
    on thee;
Nor untwist – slack they may be – these last
    strands of man
In me ór, most weary, cry *I can no more*. I can;
Can something, hope, wish day come, not choose
    not to be.

But ah, but O thou terrible, why wouldst thou
    rude on me
They wring-world right foot rock? lay a lionlimb
    against me? scan
With darksome devouring eyes my bruisèd bones?
    and fan,
O in turns of tempest, me heaped there; me
    frantic to avoid thee and flee?

Why? That my chaff might fly; my grain lie, sheer
    and clear.
Nay in all that toil, that coil, since (seems) I
    kissed the rod,
Hand rather, my heart lo! lapped strength, stole
    joy, would laugh, chéer.
Cheer whom though? The hero whose heaven-
    handling flung me, fóot tród
Me? or me that fought him? O which one? is it
    each one? That night, that year
Of now done darkness I wretch lay wrestling with
    (my God!) my God.

No worst, there is none. Pitched past pitch of grief,
More pangs will, schooled at forepangs, wilder
   wring.
Comforter, where, where is your comforting?
Mary, mother of us, where is your relief?
My cries heave, herds-long; huddle in a main, a
   chief-
woe, world-sorrow; on an age-old anvil wince and
   sing –
Then lull, then leave off. Fury had shrieked 'No ling-
ering! Let me be fell: force I must be brief'.
O the mind, mind has mountains; cliffs of fall
Frightful, sheer, no-man-fathomed. Hold them
   cheap
May who ne'er hung there. Nor does long our small
Durance deal with that steep or deep. Here! creep,
Wretch, under a comfort serves in a whirlwind: all
Life death does end and each day dies with sleep.

I wake and feel the fell of dark, not day.
What hours, O what black hoürs we have spent
This night! what sights you, heart, saw; ways you
     went!
And more must, in yet longer light's delay.

With witness I speak this. But where I say
Hours I mean years, mean life. And my lament
Is cries countless, cries like dead letters sent
To dearest him that lives alas! away.

I am gall, I am heartburn. God's most deep decree
Bitter would have me taste: my taste was me;
Bones built in me, flesh filled, blood brimmed the
     curse.

Selfyeast of spirit a dull dough sours. I see
The lost are like this, and their scourge to be
As I am mine, their sweating selves; but worse.

My own heart let me more have pity on; let
Me live to my sad self hereafter kind,
Charitable; not live this tormented mind
With this tormented mind tormenting yet.

I cast for comfort I can no more get
By groping round my comfortless, than blind
Eyes in their dark can day or thirst can find
Thirst's all-in-all in all a world of wet.

Soul, self; come, poor Jackself, I do advise
You, jaded, let be; call off thoughts awhile
Elsewhere; leave comfort root-room; let joy size

At God knows when to God knows what; whose
      smile
's not wrung, see you; unforeseen times rather – as
      skies
Betweenpie mountains – lights a lovely mile.

Justus quidem tu es, Domine, si disputem tecum; verumtame
justa loquar ad te: Quare via impiorum prosperatur? &c.

Thou are indeed just, Lord, if I contend
With thee; but, sir, so what I plead is just.
Why do sinners' ways prosper? and why must
Disappointment all I endeavour end?

Wert thou my enemy, O thou my friend,
How wouldst thou worse, I wonder, than thou dost
Defeat, thwart me? Oh, the sots and thralls of lust
Do in spare hours more thrive than I that spend,

Sir, life upon thy cause. See, banks and brakes
Now, leavèd how thick! lacèd they are again
With fretty chervil, look, and fresh wind shakes

Them; birds build – but not I build; no, but strain,
Time's eunuch, and not breed one work that wakes.
Mine, O thou lord of life, send my roots rain.

NOTES ON THE PICTURES

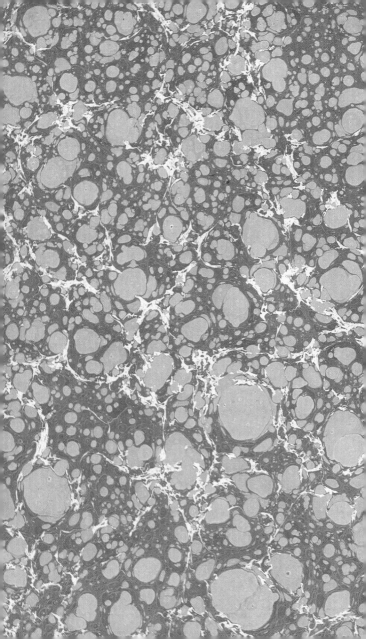